DRAWING

STYLES AND TECHNIQUES

This edition published in 2015
By SpiceBox™
12171 Horseshoe Way
Richmond, BC
Canada V7A 4V4

First published in 2010
Copyright © SpiceBox™ 2010

ISBN 10: 1-77132-013-3
ISBN 13: 978-1-77132-013-9

CEO and Publisher: Ben Lotfi
Editorial: AnnMarie MacKinnon
Creative Director: Garett Chan
Art Director: Christine Covert
Design & Layout: Leslie Irvine & Kirsten Reddecopp
Production: James Badger & Mell D'Clute
Sourcing: Janny Lam, Jin Xiong

For more SpiceBox products and information, visit our website:
www.spiceboxbooks.com

Manufactured in China

5 7 9 10 8 6

CONTENTS

INTRODUCTION

This is just the book for aspiring artists who want to learn and develop skills—with it you'll have an opportunity to explore the art of drawing, to investigate all the exciting possibilities. Perhaps in reading and trying the exercises, you'll find some of the spark that generates enthusiasm. Much can be learned by checking out the approach of the many other artists in the examples provided. Certainly this is a book on techniques, but it is also about inspiration, the "why" of what you want to achieve as well as the "how."

Developing artistic skills requires persistence, a lot of practice—and the ability to both recognize, and learn from, the inevitable errors made in the process. Try to correct mistakes as soon as you see them. Learning to assess your ability and which areas need improvement will help to make you more objective about your work. All this takes time, and your new knowledge and skills will develop only with a good deal of hard work. Be patient . . .

And remember that the time you spend altering your drawings to improve them is never lost or wasted. It is the foundation of your future role as an artist. As you progress, it will be very satisfying to see the improvement in your skills as the drawings come closer to achieving your aims.

This need not be a lonely or private process. In fact, making contact with other people who are also trying to become better artists will help you progress. Share your work with others. Your best critics will be other students of art who understand what you are experiencing and trying to achieve.

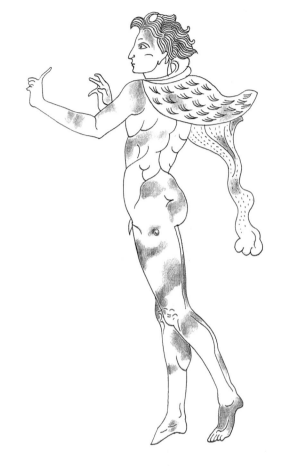

If you know any professional artists, talk to them about their work and seek their advice and direction. However, while you do need to be aware of your weaknesses in order to try to maximize your skills, never ignore your strengths. These are what you must build upon to achieve success. Meanwhile, it may also be helpful to visit art shows and galleries for extra inspiration and motivation.

Whatever your ultimate aims—as you start and refine your skills—this book will help you to explore an exciting media and may be the stepping stone to many artistic endeavors.

Enjoy the experience.

Line and style: The loose and yet taut line evident in the copy of Matisse's odalisque (page 4) can take years to perfect, but there is no reason why you should not try to produce something similar now —it will enormously improve your drawing skills.

A vivid sense of style will give even a line drawing its own vitality. The simple but original design of this cut-out bronze figure from the Hellenic period (above) is outstanding.

WHAT YOU WILL DISCOVER

In the following sections, we will be looking at all kinds of drawing. Some you will be familiar with, and some will be new to you. Many of the examples are close copies of the work of well-known artists, who provide an inspiring wealth of ideas and methods. In considering the drawings of master artists and how they were done, try to relate them to your own experience of drawing and discover how they may show you ways to improve your own abilities.

Topics such as anatomy and perspective are looked at in some detail, as is the difficulty of drawing movement. Detailed on the right are the major themes running through the book and an explanation of how they can help you develop your drawing skills. Also included in the book are examples of drawings that exemplify the major topics we will explore.

Major themes
• The work of artists who found ways of seeing the world anew (see pages 31–37). In their hands, what might seem like an ordinary situation suddenly becomes full of promise and life.

• Devices and approaches that may help us to improve the accuracy of our drawing (see pages 38–41). We'll also consider how to analyze the mass of information thrown at our retina.

• Form, and how to produce the effect of dimension, with shapes conditioned by light and shade and other dimensional devices (see pages 43–49).

• Studying from nature (see pages 50–60). In this and other sections, you will find exercises in drawing and analysis, to understand how to see a subject more clearly and how to represent what you see.

• Throughout the learning process, it is important to draw what you can see. Not to draw what cannot be seen might seem obvious, but it is a very precise discipline for the artist with lots of ideas in his head who sometimes attempts to invent without substance. Train yourself to see more, perceive more clearly and draw exactly what is seen.

HOW YOU WILL LEARN

Different effects with brush and ink: These two landscapes give very different effects although a very similar technique was used for both.

First and foremost, the goal for this book is to allow you to have fun. If you want to learn to draw well and are prepared to put in plenty of time and practice, there is nothing to stop you.

Some of the styles and techniques will suit you instantly, whereas with others, you may find yourself having to work hard. Don't worry if you don't instantly pick all of them up. See them as a challenge. You will discover that just trying a new technique will bring improvement in the other methods you use. Seemingly difficult exercises firm up talent. When you succeed at them, you will have the satisfaction of knowing that you have achieved a new skill.

Above all, remember that your own desire to draw and the normal use of your senses are all that are required to start the deeper investigation into the visual world that this book hopes to encourage. Art is a marvelous part of life, and drawing is an essential basis for painting and sculpture—as well as a wonderful art form in its own right.

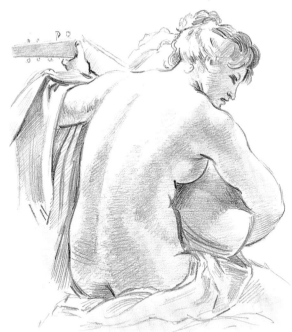

In the copy of the Vouet (left), the carefully modulated toning makes us very aware of the aesthetic value.

In the copy of the Caracci (right), you can see that it was drawn quickly. Most of the tonal lines go in the same direction and the figure looks solid and convincingly muscular.

INTRODUCTION TO TECHNIQUES

To develop an individual style and method of working, you have to experiment. This is easy, given the wide range of materials and implements widely available. Try different implements and papers and the effects that can be achieved with them—for example, various types of pencil, as well as pen and ink, line and wash, chalk, pastel, charcoal, scratchboard (a technique not used very much these days) and some very interesting, if labor-intensive, ways of making marks on paper.

In this book you'll see some of the approaches to the art of drawing taken by different artists at different times. However alien or different from your usual way of working, this experimentation gives you an opportunity to discover new techniques and approaches, and to incorporate them in your own work. Try your hand at all of them, and see if you can invent a new style. The main point is to have some fun.

Both implements and materials are important. An eager artist will draw with anything and make it work to his or her advantage. Artists feel compelled to draw, no matter what their situation. If nothing else is available, they'll use sticks in sand, coal on whitewashed walls, or colored mud on flat rocks.

It is not essential to have a wide range of equipment at your disposal. One of the things that make drawing such a popular art form is that you can begin with a minimal amount of supplies. Supply yourself with the best materials you can afford. If you try as many new tools and materials as you can, you will discover what suits you best. Some obvious basic implements are described on pages 10–12.

IMPLEMENTS AND MATERIALS

Pencil

The most simple, universal tool of the artist is the humble pencil, which is very versatile. It ranges from very hard, to very soft and black (H, HB, B, 2B, etc.) and there are differing thicknesses. Depending on the type you choose, pencil can be used very precisely and also very loosely. You should have at least three degrees of blackness, such as an HB (average hardness and blackness), 2B (soft and black), and 4B (very soft and black). For working on a toned surface, you might like to try white carbon pencil.

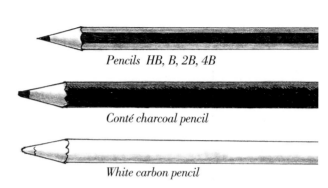

Pencils HB, B, 2B, 4B

Conté charcoal pencil

White carbon pencil

Graphite

Graphite pencils are thicker than ordinary pencils and come in an ordinary wooden casing or as solid graphite sticks with a thin plastic covering. The graphite in the plastic coating is thicker, more solid, and lasts longer, but the wooden casing probably feels better. The solid stick is very versatile because of the actual breadth of the drawing edge, enabling you to draw a really thick line as well as very fine lines. Graphite also comes in various grades, from hard to very soft and black.

graphite pencils

Pen

Dip pens come with a fine pointed nib, either stiff or flexible. Modern fine-pointed graphic pens are easier to use and less messy, but not so versatile in terms of the lines it can produce. Try both types.

The ink for dip pens is black "India ink," or drawing ink; this can be permanent or water-soluble.

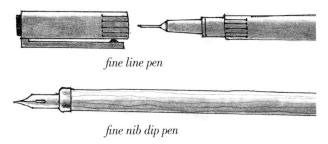

fine line pen

fine nib dip pen

Charcoal

Charcoal pencils, which come in black and gray and white, are excellent when you need to produce dimensional images on toned paper and are less messy to use than sticks of charcoal and chalk. However, the sticks are more versatile because you can use the long edge as well as the point. Drawings in this type of media need "fixing" to stop them from rubbing away, but if interleaved with pieces of paper, they can be kept without smudging. Work you wish to show for any length of time should be fixed with a spray.

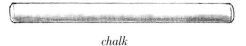

willow charcoal

Chalk

This is a cheaper and longer-lasting alternative to white Conté or white pastel.

chalk

Brush

A number 0 or number 2 nylon brush is satisfactory for drawing. For applying washes of tone, a number 6 or number 10 brush, either in sablette or sable or any other material capable of producing a good point, is recommended.

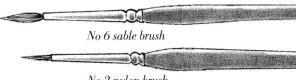

No 6 sable brush

No 2 nylon brush

11

Paper and board

Any decent, smooth drawing paper is suitable for your work. A rougher surface gives a more broken line and greater texture. Try out as many different papers as you can. For brushwork, use a modestly priced watercolor paper to start with. Most line illustrators use a smooth board, but you may find this too smooth; the pen slides across it so easily that your line is difficult to control.

Scratchboard has a layer of china clay that is thick enough to allow dry paint to be scraped off, but thin enough not to crack off. It comes in black and white. White scratchboard is the more versatile of the two, and allows the ink to be scraped with a sharp point or edge when it is dry to produce interesting textures or lines. The black version has a thin layer of black ink printed evenly over the whole surface, which can be scraped away to produce a reverse drawing resembling a woodcut or engraving. Try them out. Cut your first piece of board into smaller pieces so that you can experiment with a range of different approaches. (The more unusual techniques involving scratchboard are dealt with later in this section.) The tools you need to work effectively with scratchboard can be obtained at any good art or craft store.

Scratchboard tool

Clutch pencil with silver wire point

PENCIL DRAWING: EXAMPLE 1

Pencil drawing

Pencil can be used in many ways. When it was invented—sometime in the 17th century—it revolutionized artists' techniques because of the enormous variety of skillful effects that could be produced with it. It soon came to replace well-established drawing implements such as silverpoint.

The production of pencils in different grades of hardness and blackness greatly enhanced the medium's versatility. Now it became easy to draw in a variety of ways: delicately or vigorously, precisely or vaguely, with linear effect or with strong or soft tonal effects.

Here, we have several types of pencil drawing, from the carefully precise to the impulsively messy, from powerful, vigorous mark making to soft, sensitive shades of tone.

Looking at the works of Michelangelo is a good starting point for seeing ways of using pencil. His work was extremely skillful and his anatomical knowledge was second to none.

The careful shading of each of the muscle groups in the body gives an almost sculptural effect, which is not so surprising when you consider that sculpture was his first love. To draw like this takes time and patience and careful analysis of the figure you are drawing.

PENCIL DRAWING: EXAMPLE 2

Titian's knowledge of color was so good that even his drawings look as though they were painted. He is obviously feeling for texture and depth and movement in the space and is not worried about defining anything too tightly. The lines merge and cluster together to make a very powerful, tactile group.

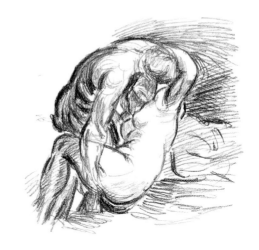

PENCIL DRAWING: EXAMPLE 3

Now look at this vigorous drawing by Delacroix, the great French Romantic artist. The powerful flowing lines show the activity and forcefulness of the figure. Where shading has been applied, it is very strongly blocked in areas of dark shadows. Handling pencil in this way requires confidence. When you are learning, it is useful sometimes just to let go and have a shot at producing a strong image. You have nothing to lose—you can always try again if your drawing goes wrong.

PENCIL DRAWING: EXAMPLE 4

This meticulous pencil drawing, by the German Julius Schnorr von Carolsfeld, is one of the most perfect drawings in this style. The result is quite stupendous, even though this is just a copy and probably doesn't have the precision of the original. Every line is visible. The tonal shading that follows the contours of the limbs is exquisitely observed. This is not at all easy to do and getting the repeated marks to line up correctly requires great discipline. It is worth practicing this kind of drawing because it will increase your skill at manipulating the pencil and test your ability to concentrate.

PENCIL DRAWING: EXAMPLE 5

The simple outline
In different ways, drawings may exploit a very simple outline. Such simplicity serves to "fix" the main shape of the drawing, ensuring the effect of the additional detailed shading. This much more economical method of drawing need not be at the expense of the information offered about the subjects depicted.

Both Matisse (copy of a self-portrait, right) and Victor Ambrus (bottom right) appear to have used several different grades of pencil for these drawings; some lines are very soft and black, others much less so. Knowing how far to go is an art in itself. Ambrus has achieved balance by outlining the main shape of the dog with a soft gray line and then adding details of the curly hair and dark ears, head and nose with darker, crisper lines.

PENCIL DRAWING: EXAMPLE 6

Only one of the objects in this still-life group has been drawn in great detail. The rest of them are in a bare outline drawing. This is an unfinished drawing, but does show how to achieve a convincing solidity by first drawing clearly defined outline shapes before exploring the details.

PEN AND INK: EXAMPLE 1

Pen and ink

Pen and ink is special in that once you've put the line down, it is indelible and can't be erased. This really tests an artist's ability because, unless they can use a mass of fine lines to build a form, they have to get the lines "right" the first time. Either way can work. Once you get a taste for using ink, it can be very addictive. The tension of knowing that you can't change what you have done in a drawing is challenging. When it goes well, it can be exhilarating.

Leonardo probably did the original of this as a study for a painting. Drawn fairly sketchily in simple line, it shows a young woman with a unicorn, a popular courtly device of the time. The lines are sensitive and loose, but the whole hangs together very beautifully with the minimal of drawing. The use of minimal shading in a few oblique lines to suggest

areas of tone is just enough to convey the artist's intentions.

PEN AND INK: EXAMPLE 2

This copy of a Raphael work is more heavily shaded in a variety of crosshatching, giving much more solidity to the figures despite the slightly fairytale imagery. The movement is conveyed nicely, and the body of the rider looks very substantial as he cuts down the dragon. The bits of background lightly put in give even more strength to the figures of knight, horse, and dragon.

PEN AND INK: EXAMPLE 3

This next copy, of a Michelangelo drawing, is much more heavily worked over, with hefty crosshatching capturing the muscularity of the figure.

The texture is rich and gives a very good impression of a powerful, youthful figure. The left arm and the legs are unfinished, but even so, the drawing has great impact.

PEN AND INK: EXAMPLE 4

Rarely has there been such brilliant line drawing in ink of the human figure as those of the painter Guercino. In this example, the line is extremely economical and looks as though it has been drawn from life very rapidly. The flowing lines seem to produce the effect of a solid body in space, but they also have a marvelous lyrical quality of their own.

Try drawing like this, quickly without worrying about anything except the most significant details, but getting the feel of the subject in as few lines as possible. You will have to draw something directly from life in order to get an understanding of how this technique works.

PEN AND INK: EXAMPLE 5

In his masterly original of this drawing in line (and ink), Tintoretto was careful to get the whole outline of the figure. The curvy interior lines suggest the muscularity of the form. There is not too much detail, but just enough to convince the eye of the powerful body; every muscle here appears to ripple under the skin. The barest of shading suggests the form.

PEN AND INK: EXAMPLE 6

The head below shows the importance of
background when attempting to describe
the way form builds around a rounded object.
Some areas have been left clear to suggest
light catching the hair, ears, nose, etc., and
these stand out against the crosshatched
background tone.

To practice this technique, try it on small areas
initially. The aim is to learn to control your
pen strokes so that you can lay them closely
together without them becoming jumbled. You
will need several attempts to make the lines
go only over the areas you want. Try drawing
in the main shape with pencil first, and then
ink over it so that you have pencil lines up to
which to draw.

LINE ON WASH: EXAMPLE 1

Now we move on to look at the effects that can be obtained
by using a mixture of pen and brush with ink. The lines
are usually drawn first to get the main shape of the subject,
then a brush loaded with ink and water is used to float
across certain areas to suggest shadow and fill in most of
the background to give depth.

A good-quality solid paper is necessary for this type of
drawing; try either a watercolor paper or a very heavy
drawing paper. The wateriness of the tones needs to be
calculated to the area to be covered. In other words, don't
make it so wet that the paper takes ages to dry.

This copy of a Rembrandt is very dramatic in its use of
light and shade.

LINE ON WASH: EXAMPLE 2

When using line and wash in landscape drawing, the handling of the wash is particularly important, because its different tonal values suggest space receding into the picture plane. Here we look at two drawings by Claude Lorrain.

This sensitive pen line drawing of part of an old Roman ruin has a light wash of watery ink to suggest the sun shining from behind the stones. The wash has been kept uniform. The outlines of the stone blocks give you lines up to which to draw.

These two deer are fairly loosely drawn in black chalk. A variety of tones of wash have been freely splashed across the animals to suggest form and substance.

LINE ON WASH: EXAMPLE 3

Master landscape painter Claude Lorrain gives a real lesson in how to draw nature in this study of a tree. Executed with much feeling but great economy, the whole drawing is done in brushwork. To try this you need three different sizes of brush (try Nos. 0 or 1, 6 and 10), all of them with good points. Put in the lightest areas first (very dilute ink), then the medium tones (more ink less water), and then the very darkest (not quite solid ink).

Notice how Lorrain doesn't try to draw each leaf, but makes interesting blobs and scrawls with the tip of the brush to suggest a leafy canopy. With the heavier tones, he allows the brush to cover larger areas and in less detail. He blocks in some very dark areas with the darkest tone and returns to the point of the brush to describe branches and some clumps of leaf.

CHALK ON TONE: EXAMPLE 1

The use of toned paper can bring an extra dimension to a drawing and is very effective at producing a three-dimensional effect of light and shade. Whether you are drawing with chalk, pastel, or charcoal, it's very important to remember that the paper itself is in effect an implement, providing all the tones between the extremes of light and dark. Resist the temptation to completely obliterate the toned paper in your enthusiasm to cover the whole area with chalk marks.

Below, the mid-tone of the paper has been used to great effect in this copy of Carpaccio's drawing of a Venetian merchant. Small marks of white chalk pick out the parts of garments, face, and hair that catch the light. No attempt has been made to connect these marks. The dark chalk has been used similarly: as little as the artist felt he could get away with. The medium tone of the paper becomes the solid body that registers the bright lights falling on the figure. The darkest tones give the weight and the outline of the head.

CHALK ON TONE: EXAMPLE 2

As we have seen in the examples on the previous page, the use of toned paper reduces the area that has to be covered with chalk and heightens the effect of the chalk marks, especially if these have been made in white. The illustrations shown here exemplify the range of effects that can be achieved with toned paper.

In Watteau's picture of a goddess (right), the dark outline emphasizes the figure and limbs, as do the patches of bright light on the upper facing surfaces.

CHALK ON TONE: EXAMPLE 3

This drawing was executed in white and dark chalk on medium-toned paper. The approach taken is about as economical as you can get. The form of the surface of the girl's face and figure is barely hinted at down one side, with just the slightest amount of chalk. A similar effect is achieved on the other side, this time in dark chalk. The uncovered paper does much of the rest of the work.

CHALK ON TONE: EXAMPLE 4

The second drawing takes the use of dark and light much further, creating a substantial picture. In places, the white chalk is piled on, and elsewhere, is barely visible. The dark chalk is handled in the same way. More of the toned paper is covered, but its contribution to the overall effect of the drawing is not diminished.

CHALK ON TONE: EXAMPLE 5

The French neo-classicist master Pierre Paul Prud'hon was a brilliant worker in the medium of chalk on toned paper. In these copies of examples of his work, he shows us two very effective ways of using light and dark tones to suggest form.

In this drawing of Psyche, marks have been made with dark and light chalk, creating a texture of light that is rather Impressionistic in flavor. The lines, which are mostly quite short, go in all directions. The impression created is of a figure in the dark. This is helped by the medium tone of the paper, which almost disappears under the pattern of the mark making.

CHALK ON TONE: EXAMPLE 6

The chalk marks in this close up are much disciplined. A whole range of tones is built from the carefully controlled marks, which show off the form as though lit from above. Here, too, the middle tone is mostly covered over with gradations of black and white.

SCRATCHBOARD: EXAMPLE 1

Scratchboard drawing evolved during the early days of photographic reproduction in newspapers as a response to the needs of advertisers, who wanted to show their wares and products to best advantage but were limited by the poor quality of the printing processes then available. The technique gave very clear, precise definition to photographs, and so became the means of rendering advertisements for newsprint.

Over time, of course, the screen printing of photographs improved so much that scratchboard has become just another art technique. It does have some qualities of its own, however. It is similar in some respects to wood engraving, wood cuts, or engraving on metal, although, because of the ease of drawing, it is considered less flexible and more time-consuming.

In this drawing, the boater appearing across a misty lake or river was first sketched in pencil, then blocked out in large areas of ink. The figure of the man, the oars and the atmospherics were done in diluted ink to make a paler tone. The boat was drawn in black ink. Using a scratchboard tool, lines were carefully scratched across the tonal areas, reducing their tonal qualities further. Some areas have few or no scratched lines, giving a darker tone and an effect of dimension.

SCRATCHBOARD: EXAMPLE 2

You can see in the example below how scratchboard technique lends itself to a certain formalized way of drawing. The scratch marks can be made to look very decorative.

Scratchboard technique is similar to crosshatching with a pencil, although with the former, you are drawing white on black, of course. The surface of the board can be scratched over several times, as long as the marks have not cut too deeply into the china clay. Any areas that need to be strengthened or corrected can be filled in with ink. Correcting

lines using this technique is very easy: you just scratch out the wrong bits and redraw them.

This illustration was first drawn in black ink. The areas of ink were then gone over using the scraper tool to reduce the heaviness of the shaded areas and clean up the edges to achieve the shape required.

BLOTTING TECHNIQUE

First used by illustrators in the 1950s, this technique was made famous by Andy Warhol in his fashion illustrations. The idea is to take a piece of ordinary drawing paper, or blotting paper—either will achieve the same effect—and fold it in half. After drawing each line in ink, you blot it into the opposite side of the page. You have to take a painstaking approach, blotting as you build up the drawing, because otherwise the ink dries too quickly. A dip pen is the best tool, because modern graphic pens don't produce ink that is wet enough.

Generally, it is best to draw only a few lines at a time and then blot them immediately. If you draw too many lines before blotting them, the ink will dry and the point of using this technique will be lost. However, you have to experiment with timings and weight of line, because sometimes a pleasing effect can result from an unpromising start. In the last drawing, for example, the multiple lines on the face dried so quickly that the blotted version looked less tonal than the original but this works well. How you want your finished drawing to look is up to you.

Original drawing

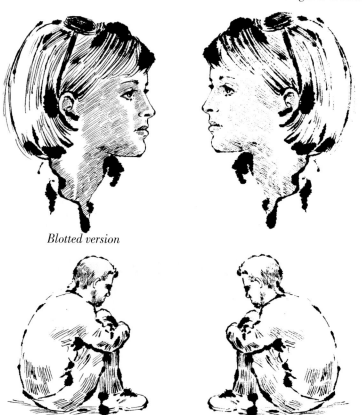

Blotted version

CARD-EDGE TECHNIQUE

This technique was invented at about the same time as the blotting technique. The first step is to cut out small pieces of thin cardboard. The edges of these are then dipped into soft wet paint (gouache designer colors are best) and used to draw lines onto a blank sheet. The effect is initially very strong, becoming fainter and fainter as the paint gets used up or dries.

Like blotting technique, it is a slow process and you cannot produce much in the way of curved shapes, but the end result can be very powerful.

In terms of how it is used and the effects that can be achieved with it, it is somewhat similar to painting with a palette knife.

In this example, the gouache on the edge of the cardboard was almost dry when it was used to paint the clouds and front surface of the house. For the roof and dark trees in the background, the cardboard was very wet and full of paint.

SILVERPOINT

The last technique to be attempted is silverpoint drawing. This classic method, used before pencils were invented, produces very precise, refined drawings. Many drawings by Renaissance artists were made in this way.

First, you have to buy a piece of silver wire—try a jeweler or someone who deals in precious metals—about one 25th of an inch (1 mm) thick and about 3 inches (75 mm) long. This is either held in a wooden handle taped to it or within a clutch-action propelling pencil that takes wire of this thickness.

Cover a piece of drawing paper (use fairly thick paper because it is less likely to buckle) with a wash of permanent white gouache designer paint; the coat must cover the whole surface and shouldn't be either too thick or too watery. When the white paint has dried, you draw onto it with the silver wire; ensure that the end of the wire is smooth and rounded to prevent it tearing the paper. Don't press too hard. The silver deposits a very fine silky line, like a pencil, but lasts much longer.

To use silverpoint, you need to prepare the background first. Here, white paint (mixed with a bit of reddish-brown) was applied and dried before the silver was used.

DRAWING YOUR WORLD

Keep a sketchpad with you always—you never know when you'll stumble across a scene that you want to put down on paper.

Before you begin, it's worthwhile to review these hints about methods of practice and good habits.

One invaluable practice is to draw regularly from life. That is, draw the objects, people, landscapes, and details around you. These have an energy and atmosphere that only personal engagement with them can capture. Photographs or other representations are inadequate substitutes and should be used only as a last resort as reference.

Always have a sketchbook or two and use them as often as possible. Constant sketching will sharpen your drawing skills and keep them honed. Gather plenty of materials and tools— pencils, pens, erasers, sharpeners, ink, paper of all kinds—and invest in a portfolio to contain all your drawings.

Successful drawing does not demand a sophisticated or complex approach.

Look at this sketch. Its quality derives from a simple approach to shapes and the assimilation of their graphic effects into one picture.

Always make an effort to keep shapes basic and simple in your drawings.

Don't throw away your drawings for at least a year after you've finished them. At that distance, you can be more objective about their merits or failings, and have a clear idea of which ones work and which ones don't. In the white-hot creative moment, you don't actually know whether what you've done is any good or not. You are too attached to your end result. Later on, you'll be more detached and be clearer in your judgment.

Build a portfolio of work and sometimes mount your drawings. Then, if anyone wants to see your work, you will have something to show them. Don't be afraid of letting people see what you have done. People always find drawings interesting. Have fun with what you are doing, and enjoy your investigations of the visual world.

The quick sketches of different parts of buildings above are the result of drawing often and at any time. There is always the possibility of making a sketch of something seen out of a window. This is very good practice, too.

DRAWING FROM THE MASTERS: ANCIENT GREEKS

The point of this section is not to encourage you to blindly copy the methods of Raphael or Leonardo or any of the other great masters whose works we'll be looking at. The most important aspect of drawing at this level is the acute observation that it requires. Great artists observe the world around them with accuracy.

From these examples, try to begin to understand how to put technique at the service of your observations by varying the length and pressure of your strokes. Eventually, after a lot of practice, you will find that you can judge exactly how heavy, light, long, or short your strokes should be to achieve a specific effect. You'll also find that you can get quite fast at it the more you practice. One of the great bonuses of studying drawing and painting is that our vision refines and we begin to drop the prejudices and preconceptions that normally accompany our view of the world—we gain attributes that are abundantly in evidence in the work of the artists whose methods we look at in this section.

Ancient Greek Art

The Greek vase drawings above, some of the earliest known (dating from c. 510 BC), are so sophisticated and elegant they might have been drawn by a modern-day Picasso or Matisse, except that Matisse would not have been as exact and Picasso would probably not have been as anatomically correct. The simple incised line appears to have been done easily and quickly and yet must have been the result of years of practice. Yet more remarkable is that these drawings were not done on flat paper, but on the curving surface of a vase or crater. The economy of line is a lesson to all aspiring artists.

DRAWING FROM THE MASTERS: LEONARDO DA VINCI

Leonardo da Vinci (1459–1519)

When we look at a Leonardo drawing, we see the immense talent of an artist who could not only see more clearly than most of us, but also had the technical ability to express it on paper. We see the ease of the strokes of silverpoint or chalk, outlining the various parts of the design, some sharply defined and others soft, and in multiple marks that give the impression of the surface moving around the shape and disappearing from view.

Leonardo regulates light and shade by means of his famous sfumato method (Italian for "evaporated"), a technique by which an effect of depth and volume is achieved by the use of dark, misty tones. The careful grading of the dark, smudgy marks helps us to see how the gradations of tone give the appearance of three dimensions.

The effect of dimension is also shown with very closely drawn lines that appear as a surface, and are so smoothly, evenly drawn that our eyes are convinced. There is elegance in the way he puts in enough tone but never too much. To arrive at this level of expertise requires endless practice. However, it is worth persevering with practicing techniques because they enable you to produce what you want with greater ease. Techniques need to be mastered and then forgotten. All this will take time.

DRAWING FROM THE MASTERS: RAPHAEL

Raphael (Raffaelo Sanzio) (1483–1520)

The perfection of Raphael's drawings must have seemed quite extraordinary to his contemporaries, even though they had already seen the works of Filippo Lippi, Botticelli, Michelangelo, and Leonardo. His exquisitely flowing lines show his mastery as a draftsman; notice the apparent ease with which he outlines the forms of his Madonna and Child, and how few lines he needs to show form, movement, and even the emotional quality of the figures he draws. His loosely drawn lines describe a lot more than we notice at first glance. It is well worth trying to copy his simplicity, even though your attempts may fall far short of the original. The originals are unrepeatable, and it is only by studying them at first hand that you will begin to understand exactly how his handling of line and tone is achieved.

DRAWING FROM THE MASTERS: HANS HOLBEIN

Hans Holbein the Younger (1497/8–1543)

Holbein left behind some extraordinarily subtle portrait drawings of various courtiers whom he painted during his time as court painter to Henry VIII. These works are now in the Queen's Collection (most of them at Windsor, in England, but some are in the Queen's Gallery at Buckingham Palace), and are worth studying for their brilliant subtle modeling. These subjects have no wrinkles to show their character, and their portraits are like those of children, with very little to show other than the shape of the head, the eyes, nostrils, mouth and hair. Holbein has achieved this quality by drastically reducing the modeling of the form and putting in just enough information to make the eye accept his untouched areas as the surfaces of the face. We tend to see what we expect to see. A good artist uses this to his advantage. So, less is more.

DRAWING FROM THE MASTERS: EDGAR DEGAS

Edgar Degas (1834–1917)

Degas was taught by a pupil of Ingres, and studied drawing in Italy and France until he was the most expert draftsman of all the Impressionists. His loose flowing lines (often repeated several times to get the exact feel) look simple but are inordinately difficult to master. The skill evident in his paintings and drawings came out of continuous practice. He declared that his epitaph should be: "He greatly loved drawing." He would often trace and retrace his own drawings in order to get the movement and grace he was after. Hard work and constant efforts to improve his methods honed his natural talent.

DRAWING FROM THE MASTERS: GEORGES SEURAT

Georges Seurat (1859–91)

Seurat's style of drawing is very different from what we have seen so far; mainly because he was so interested in producing a mass or area of shape that he reduced many of his drawings to tone alone. In these pictures, there are no real lines, but large areas of graduated tone rendered in charcoal, Conté, or thick pencil on faintly grainy textured paper. Their beauty is that they convey both substance and atmosphere while leaving a lot to the viewer's imagination. The careful grading of tone is instructive, as is how one mass can be made to work against a lighter area.

DRAWING FROM THE MASTERS:
HENRI MATISSE

Henri Matisse (1869–1954)
Even without the aid of bright, rich colors, Matisse could invest his work with great sensuality. His drawings are marvelously understated yet graphic, thanks to the fluidity of line. Awkwardness is evident in some of them, but even with these, you never doubt that they express exactly what he wanted. There are no extraneous marks to diffuse the image and confuse the eye. As he got older and suffered from arthritis in his hands, Matisse resorted to drawing with charcoal on the end of a long stick. Despite this handicap, the large, simple images he produced by this method possess great power.

THE EXPERIENCES OF DRAWING: PERSPECTIVE

Perspective

There are many things to be borne in mind with perspective. The main point is that it's impossible to put down exactly what we see in the two dimensions of drawing and painting. A certain amount of adjustment and artistic license has to be allowed. A flat map can't replicate the world's surface, which is curved, and so will have to sacrifice either area shape or area proportion.

When we look at something ordinarily, our eyes scan the scene. However, when we look at a picture, our vision is drawn as though from one point. The artist, therefore, has to limit his area of vision to one that can be taken in at a glance.

The artist must also be aware of his own eye-level or where the horizon really is, however much it is obscured by hills, trees, or buildings. The actual cone or field of vision is about 60 degrees, but the artist will need to limit his picture to much less to avoid distortion.

Relationships in the picture plane

In the example shown here, we look at the relationships between the tree, post, and flowers and the horizon line. As you can see, the height of the tree in the picture appears not as high as the post, although, in reality, the post is smaller than the tree. This is due to the effect of perspective, the tree being further away than the post. There is also an area of ground between the bottom of the tree and the flower. The horizon line is the same as the eye-level of the viewer.

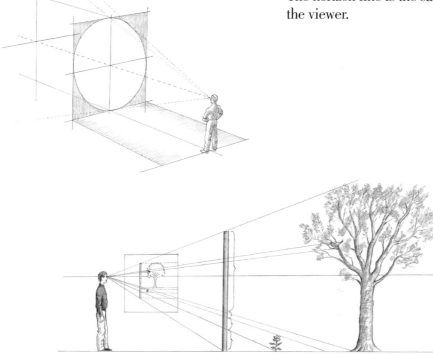

PERSPECTIVE: FIELD OF VISION

The system we look at next is quite easy to construct. You don't require training in mathematics to get it right, just the ability to use a ruler, T-square, and pair of compasses precisely. Although the picture does not have depth in reality, the eye is satisfied that it does, because it sees an area of squares that reduces geometrically as it recedes into the background.

Constructing an area of squares
Any square portions, such as floor tiles or even a checkerboard of fields, can be used to create the illusion of depth in a picture. Take one square size (A), draw in diagonal lines, and, from the crossing point of these diagonals, mark a construction line to the vanishing point.

In order to get the next rows of floor tiles related to the first correctly and in perspective, draw a line from the near corner (B) to the point where the construction line to the vanishing point cuts the far edge of the square. Continue it until it cuts the next line to the vanishing point (C) and then construct your next horizontal edge to the next tile.

Repeat in each square until you reach the point where the tiles should stop in the distance. Having produced a row of diminishing tiles, you can continue the horizontal edges of the slabs in either direction to produce the checkerboard of the floor. Notice the impressive effect you get when you fill in alternate squares.

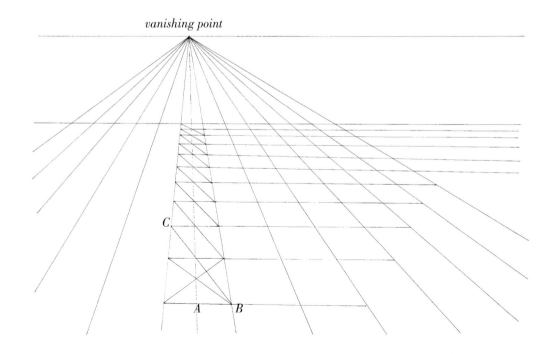

vanishing point

More about checkerboard

The kind of checkerboard floor or tiles you have been learning about has often been used in paintings to help create the illusion of depth. In early Renaissance pictures, it was thought to be amazingly realistic. These days, we are a bit more used to seeing such devices and so other effects have been brought into play to help us accept the illusion of dimensionality.

However, do experiment with the checkerboard ground—it's very simple and very effective. And don't forget to incorporate the lessons you've learned about the relationship of figure to the horizon or eyeline. If you place figures or objects on it, make sure that as they recede into the picture—standing on squares that are further back—they diminish in size consistent with your eye level (see page 38).

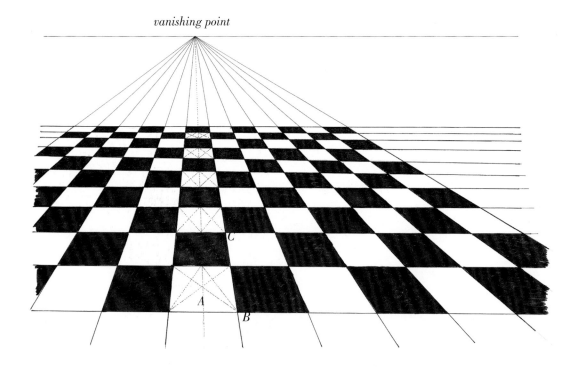

THE EXPERIENCES OF DRAWING: MOVEMENT

Movement

Drawing movement is not as difficult as it might seem at first, although it does need quite a bit of practice. You'll find it helpful if you can feel the movement you are portraying in your own body, because this will inform the movement you are trying to draw. The more you know about movement, the better. It's a good idea to observe people's movements to check out how each part of the anatomy behaves in a range of poses and attitudes.

Photographs of bodies in action are very useful, but limited in the range they offer. It is noticeable that action shots tend to capture moments of impact or of greatest force. Rarely do you find an action shot of the movements in-between. With a bit of careful observation, watching and analyzing, you should be able to see how to fill in the positions between the extremes.

Here, we see a man in the various stages of throwing a javelin. The point at which he is poised to throw and the moment when the javelin is launched are the two extremes of this process. However, you may find that drawing the man in a position between these extremes gives you a composition with more drama and tension.

Similarly here, the point between
the head completing its turn
from one side to the other
offers a different quality and
perhaps a more revealing
perspective on
the subject.

This drawing is based on a clip from a
newspaper of a rugby player kicking a
ball. It has been slightly amended from
the original to accentuate the "fuzz" of
the out-of-focus kicking foot. The speed
of this movement contrasts with the rest
of the figure, which is much more clearly
defined. The balance of the position is very
important, to accentuate the force of the
kick and the concentration of the kicker on
those distant goal posts.

FORM AND SHAPE: SHAPE RECOGNITION

Let's look at a few shapes in silhouette. What clues to identity are carried in these simple outlines?

The Spitfire is a World War II low-wing, monoplane fighter aircraft. It is easy to identify because of the particular details evident in its main frame. Similarly, the Harrier jump-jet and Sea King helicopter—aircraft that take off vertically in different ways—are not difficult to differentiate from other types of aircraft.

Our ability to recognize shapes is learned in childhood as we become aware of the wider world. Our visual vocabulary grows according to the means at our disposal from early childhood onward.

If we are to draw well, we must have the ability to connect shapes and their associations and yet differentiate between them, sometimes in quite subtle ways. Look at an object and then half close your eyes: this will reduce the impact of color and concentrate the eye on the form.

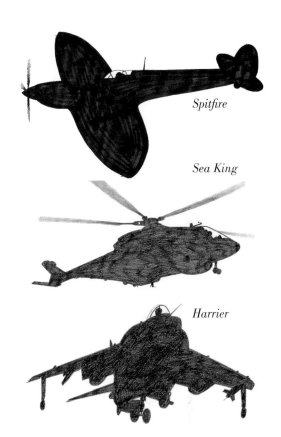

Spitfire

Sea King

Harrier

The characteristic shape of a 16th-century Spanish Morion helmet

A World War II German Army helmet

The Santa Maria, Columbus's ship

A Chinese junk

FORM AND SHAPE: CREATING FORM

Creating form

Our fairly sophisticated recognition system has to be persuaded to interpret shapes as three-dimensional forms. One way of doing this is to produce an effect that will be read as form, although in reality, this may only comprise an arrangement of lines and marks. Let's look at some examples.

A diagrammatic form is often given in atlases to represent the world. Why is it that this particular arrangement of lines inside a circle makes a fairly convincing version of a sphere with its latitude and longitude lines? We don't really think it is a sphere, but nevertheless, it carries conviction as a diagram.

Let's go a stage further. In this drawing of a bleached out photograph of an onion, the reduced striations or lines make the same point. We recognize this kind of pattern and realize that what we are looking at is intended to portray a spherical object that sprouts.

We can "see" an onion.

So is this a round fruit? No, of course not. But the drawn effect of light and shade is so familiar from our study of photographs and film that we recognize the rotund shape as a piece of fruit.

Visual conditioning: We have been educated to accept the representation of three-dimensional objects on a flat surface. This is not the case in all parts of the world. In some remote areas, for example, people cannot recognize three-dimensional objects they are familiar with from photographs.

Suggested techniques

- *Pencil / graphite p.13*
- *Pen and Ink   p.16*
- *Line & Wash   p.19*

FORM AND SHAPE: APPROACHES TO FORM

So what methods can we use to portray form convincingly so that the onlooker sees a solidity that is in fact merely inferred? Well, on these pages, we have the human figure—probably the most subtle, difficult, but most satisfying subject for drawing—and some details of the eye. These show different ways of analyzing form. Every artist has to undertake his own investigations of form. They involve methods of looking as well as methods of drawing, and through practicing them, you educate the eye, hand, and mind.

The most formidable task confronting any artist is how to draw the three-dimensional human form convincingly in one way or another.

The work of Franz Stück is linear in style; the bulk of the form above is realized with very few lines, allowing our mind to fill in the empty spaces with the fullness of the flesh.

The exampleon the right, also a copy of a Stück, is more dramatically drawn. Although the edges are soft there is a powerful fullness of form, with chalky looking tonal marks indicating the roundness of the body.

Otto Greiner's approach to form is essentially that of the classical artist, as this copy shows,

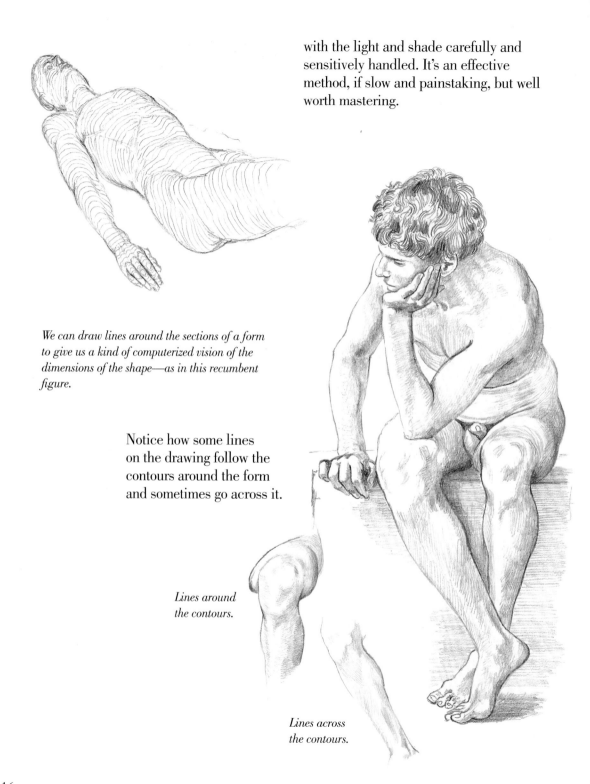

with the light and shade carefully and
sensitively handled. It's an effective
method, if slow and painstaking, but well
worth mastering.

*We can draw lines around the sections of a form
to give us a kind of computerized vision of the
dimensions of the shape—as in this recumbent
figure.*

Notice how some lines
on the drawing follow the
contours around the form
and sometimes go across it.

*Lines around
the contours.*

*Lines across
the contours.*

FORM AND SHAPE: REALIZING FORM

Exercises: realizing form
We now look at the kind of exercises that will help you to begin to see how to realize form with some power. They are all difficult, but extremely useful and very satisfying when you begin to make them work. It will require repeated practice, of course, but if you want to be an effective artist, there is no avoiding hard work.

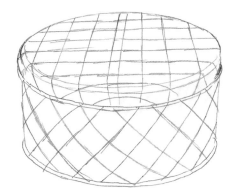

A geometric pattern on a three-dimensional shape is a marvelous exercise for the draftsman, and shows how a linear device on a surface can describe the form of that surface.

This tartan-patterned cookie tin presents various problems. The first is drawing the outline with its elliptical top and cylindrical sides. Secondly, the pattern, which proceeds around the curved edge of the tin, must be shown flat on the lid with some perspective.

Draw your outline with the basic pattern inscribed, as shown. Even without the addition of tone or detail, this gives some idea of the roundness of the sides and the flatness of the top.

With this cup and saucer, the printed landscape is tricky but interesting. You have to get the details of the printing exactly marked around the curve of the cup, otherwise the cup will look flat.

One thing that makes it a bit easier is the fact that some of the details in the pattern are not clear, and so a few mistakes won't necessarily make much difference. The main point to observe is the way the picture reduces in width as it curves around the cup.

The general outline gives the basic shape and some indication of the scene around the curved surfaces of both cup and saucer. But it is not until more detail is added with variations in tone that the roundness of the cup becomes evident.

Suggested techniques

- *Pencil / graphite*   *p.13*
- *Pen and Ink*   *p.16*
- *Line & Wash*   *p.19*

FORM AND SHAPE: REALIZING FORM

Another testing exercise is to draw an elderly human face in detail, with all the lines, textures, and marks produced by old age. If this is too difficult with a human model (it does take a long time, and your model may get restless), try drawing from a detailed close-up photograph.

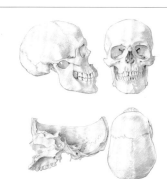

This drawing of the famous pioneer of photography, Alfred Stieglitz, was done from a photograph taken by one of his pupils. The detail in that original is brilliant and it is quite a tour-de-force to produce it in pencil or ink. You'll find that you have to discipline yourself to produce every little ripple of flesh and tuft of hair with many small, careful marks. Allow yourself plenty of time for this exercise.

Human anatomy is perhaps the ultimate test for the draftsman. If you want to excel at portrait drawing, it's worth trying to acquire a model of a skull or the use of one from a medical person or another older artist who might have access to one. Carefully draw it from different angles in great detail. Don't hurry, be precise, rub out any mistakes, re-draw ruthlessly, and don't be satisfied until the drawing is almost photographic in detail.

This example is a skull that can be taken apart, although in the complete view, the lines of division and the hooks that hold the parts together have been left out. The interior of the skull is a particularly tough challenge because it is unfamiliar to most of us. Keep the drawing precise and clean looking, so that you have no difficulty in seeing where you go wrong. This will make it easier to correct your mistakes.

Suggested techniques

- *Pencil*   *p.13*
- *Pen and Ink*   *p.16*
- *Scratchboard*   *p.24*

STUDYING LIFE FROM NATURE: PLANTS AND FLOWERS

The essential structure of a plant is not difficult to see if you study it for a time. Take a group of leaved plants: you soon notice how one type will have leaves in clusters that spring up at the points of the leaves, whereas in another, the leaves will hang down around a central point. Some plants have stalks coming off the branches evenly at the same point, others have the stalks staggered alternately down the length of the stem. Once you are familiar with a plant's characteristic shape and appearance, you will begin to notice similar properties in other plants. Observation will lend truth and conviction to even your most casual sketches. Look at the examples of plants here, noting both their similarities and differences.

The easiest way to study plants is by sketching them as often as you can. Before you begin to draw, look at the plant closely. Look at it from above, to see the leaves radiating out from the center; and from the side to see the different appearance of the leaf shapes as they project toward you, away from you, and to each side as they spiral around the stem. Note the texture of the leaves, and how it compares with that of other plants. When your subject is a flower head, draw it from an angle, whereby you can see the pattern of the petals around the center of the blossom or a profile view of them.

The appearance of the tulip is very formal and upright, with its closed cuplike flower and long, stiff stalk and leaves.

The sedum has a beautiful spiraling arrangement of leaves that curves up into a dish-like form. Rain must fill up the hollow of the leaf and run down the stalk to water the plant's roots.

The more you draw plants, the more details you will notice and the broader your vocabulary will become. After you have been drawing plants for a while, try drawing one from memory.

This exercise helps to sustain the image that your senses have recorded and will help you to memorize shapes and textures. You will find drawing from memory gives a simpler result than drawing from life, because you tend to leave out unnecessary details. The ability to produce a conventional shape easily without reference is a great asset. Once you have this ability, you will be able to bring a greater sense of realism to your drawings.

Here we have two blooms from the same plant (a clematis) at different stages of its growth. The difference is quite dramatic.

The clematis captured as it is just opening, with its smooth looking petals hanging down.

The fully open bloom, center showing to the sun: by this stage, the edges of the petals are quite crinkly.

STUDYING LIFE FROM NATURE: TREES

Growth patterns

Drawing trees has always been a favorite challenge to artists. Trees are such splendid plants, and often very beautiful, but they are not that easy to draw well. Before you begin, consider the sketches on this page.

Shapes

Getting a feel for the whole shape of the tree you want to draw is important. Often the best way to approach this is to draw in a vague outline of the main shape first. Then you need to divide this up into the various clumps of leaves and give some indication of how the main branches come off the trunk and stretch out to the final limit of the shape.

Of course, if your subject is a deciduous tree in winter, the network of branches will provide the real challenge. The branches are a maze of shapes, and success can be achieved only if you manage to analyze the main thrust of their growth and observe how the smaller branches and twigs hive off from the main structure. Luckily, trees don't move around too much, and so are excellent "sitters."

Have a look at the bigger trees in your backyard or local park or, if you're lucky enough to live in the country, in your local woods. Notice the strength of the root structure when it is evident above ground, like great, gnarled hands clutching at the earth. Next, look closely at the bark on the main trunk and branches, then at its texture. Make sketches of what you see.

These three types of deciduous tree present very different shapes and textures. Discover for yourself how different they are by finding an example of each, observing each one closely, and then spending time drawing the various shapes. Note the overall shapes and the branch patterns.

Oak

Horse Chestnut

Beech

STUDYING LIFE FROM NATURE: THE HEAD

When a person is presented as a subject, the obvious approach is to sit them down in a good light, look at them head on, and begin to draw. However, the obvious does not always produce the best or most accurate result. If you concentrate solely on getting a likeness of a subject, you miss out on the most important and most interesting aspects of portrait drawing.

The aim of this next exercise is to encourage you to look at the head as a whole. There's much more to the head than mere features, as you will discover if you look at it from many different angles, excluding the obvious one. Take a look at the two drawings shown here.

Once you have looked at various heads of different people, you will begin to classify them as whole shapes or structures and not just as faces. This approach teaches that although there are many different faces, many heads share a similar structure. The individual differences won't seem half so important once you realize that there are only a few types of heads, and each of us has a type that conforms to one of these. If you want to fully investigate this phenomenon, get your models to pose with their heads at as many different angles as possible, and explore the structure of what you see.

Suggested techniques
- *Pencil*   *p.13*
- *Pen and Ink*   *p.16*
- *Chalk on tone*   *p.21*

The head leaning back:
this angle gives a clear view of underneath
the chin and the nose, both areas we rarely
notice ordinarily. Seen from this angle, the
person is no longer instantly recognizable,
because the forehead has disappeared and
the hair is mostly behind the head.

Notice the large area of neck and chin, and
the nostrils, which are coming toward the
viewer. See how the nose sticks up out of
the main shape of the head. When seen
at this angle, the ears seem to be in a very
odd position, and their placement can be
quite tricky. Notice that the eyes no longer
dominate the head.

The head looking downward:
notice how the eyes disappear partly under
the brow; how the eyelashes stick out more
noticeably; how the nose tends to hide the
mouth and the chin almost disappears.

STUDYING LIFE FROM NATURE: HANDS

Hands are relatively easy to study, especially if you use your own as models. If you equip yourself with a mirror, you should be able to look at them from almost any angle. Of course, it will also be necessary to look at the hands of an older or younger person and also one of the opposite sex. You will find there are significant differences in shape depending on age and sex.

Always start off by observing the main structure of the hand, based on the bones underneath, and then carefully observe the hardness or softness of the flesh and skin. The

back of the hand gives the clearest indication of the age of your model. Older hands have more prominent veins and looser, more wrinkled skin around the knuckles. The hands of small children seem smooth all over.

Suggested techniques

- *Pencil*   *p.13*
- *Pen and Ink*   *p.16*
- *Chalk on tone*   *p.21*

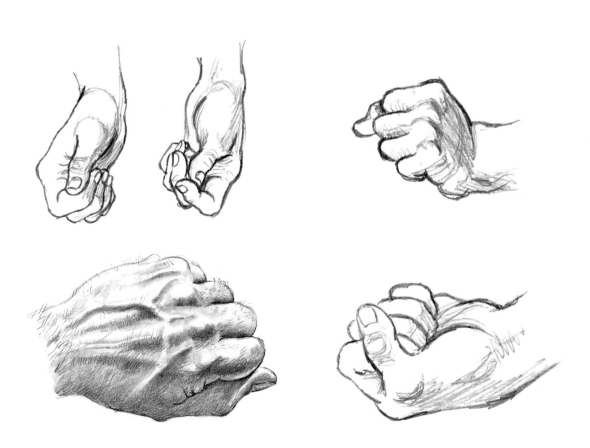

STUDYING LIFE FROM NATURE: MUSCULATURE

All human bodies have a tendency toward either a harder or softer muscularity, and both characteristics can make quite a difference to the effect of your finished picture. Look at the examples shown here.

In a hard, muscular body, the distinction between the muscles is clear and the angularity of the form has a much more active or even aggressive quality. This quality is accentuated if the bone structure is also prominent. Even in the female figure, which tends to be more restful in shape than the male, when it is lean and bony, it has this rather active or awkward look.

A soft, undulating figure, where the differences between the joining parts of the muscles are not very obvious, gives a very smooth, rounded appearance to the form, and this has an effect of calmness or weightiness. When the flesh is too heavy, the weight tends to look more awkward and so is less indicative of calm. Generally, though, softer bodies look more restful than harder ones.

Suggested techniques

- *Pencil/charcoal*   *p.13*
- *Pen and ink*   *p.16*
- *Chalk on tone*   *p.21*

STUDYING LIFE FROM NATURE: CLOTHING

Next, we look at clothing and how the movement and actions of the wearer affect it. Of course, how an item of clothing behaves will depend on the type of material from which it is made, so you need to be aware of different properties and characteristics and how to render them realistically in various situations.

This girl dancer is swirling a length of thin, light silken material. The movement of the hair and garment tell you quite a bit about her movements and type of hair and cloth.

A bit of clever posing by a fashion photographer was responsible for the original from which this drawing was made. The model was actually photographed lying on the floor with the dress spread out to make it look as though she was moving in a smooth-flowing dance. The photograph was taken in the 1930s, before the benefits of high-speed cameras and film, and represents an imaginative way around a technical problem. It proves that you can cheat the eye.

Here are three drawings of different types of
clothing, showing vastly different effects of
folds and creases, mainly due to the nature
of the material used in each case.

The raincoat sleeve shown below is similar
in character to our first example: a stiff
material made to repel water, this one has
a very smooth sheen. The folds are large,
the sleeve being loose enough to allow ease
of movement. Even in this drawing, they
look as though they would totally disappear
when the arm was straightened.

These jeans, made of tough
hard-wearing cotton, crease
easily and characteristically,
and the creases remain even
when the cloth is moved.

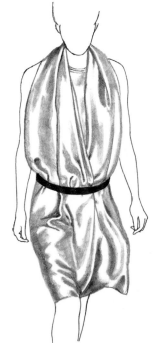

This couture garment is made of heavy satin and tailored
to keep the folds loose and mainly vertical. The movement
is not extreme and so the weight and smoothness of the
material ensure an elegant effect. When you come to
draw this type of material, be sure to get a strong contrast
between dark and light to capture the bright reflective
quality of the garment.

STUDYING LIFE FROM NATURE: EARTH

When drawing the solid rocks that make up the surface of the world, it can be instructive to think small and "build up." Pick up a handful of soil or gravel and take it home with you for close scrutiny, then try to draw it in some detail. You will find that those tiny pieces of irregular material are essentially rocks in miniature. You can get a very clear idea of how to draw the earth in all its guises by recognizing the essential similarities between earth materials and being prepared to take a jump from almost zero to infinity.

If we attempt to draw a rocky outcrop or the rocks by the sea or along the shore of a river, it is really no different from drawing small pieces of gravel, only with an enormous change of scale. It is as though those pieces of gravel have been super-enlarged. You will find a similar random mixture of shapes, though made more attractive to our eyes because of the increase in size.

One more step is to visit a mountainous area and look at the earth in its grandest, most monumental form. This example has the added quality of being above the snow-line and showing marvelously simplified icy structures against contrasting dark rocks.

STUDYING LIFE FROM NATURE: WATER

The character and mood of water changes depending on how it is affected by movement and light. Over the next few pages, we look at water in various forms, which present very different problems for artists and very different effects on viewers. To understand how you can capture the effect of each of the forms shown here requires close first-hand study, supported by photographic evidence of what is happening, followed by persistent efforts to draw what you think you know.

Here, the water is still and reflective, but even on smooth water, a breeze or currents cause small shallow ripples. Seen from an oblique angle, these ripples give a slightly broken effect along the edges of any objects reflected in the water. Try to gently blur or break the edges of each large reflected tone to simulate the rippling effect of the water.

The detailed drawing below is of a stretch of water rippling gently. There appear to be three different tones for the smooth elliptical shapes breaking the surface. This is not an easy exercise, but it will teach you something about what you actually see when looking at the surface of water.

Suggested techniques

- *Pencil*   *p.13*
- *Line on wash*   *p.19*
- *Scratchboard*   *p.21*

A waterfall is an immensely powerful form of water. It can help to observe the sight from a distance to make some sense of it. This drawing is successful largely because the watery area has been left almost blank within the enclosing rocks, trees, and other vegetation. The dark tones of the vegetation throw forward the negative shapes of the water, making them look foaming and fast moving.

BUILDING A CARICATURE

The process of turning a perfectly normal looking person into a cartoon figure to accentuate their traits is the same whether the subject is familiar to millions of households or just one. It can be a fun exercise.

The subject here is a young man. His features are perfectly normal, but they can be accentuated to bring out personality. Let's begin the process.

1. It is a good idea first to draw the person you wish to caricature several times, to get to know the shapes of his or her features and how these relate to each other.

2. Here, the young man's way of staring intensely has been slightly exaggerated along with his bony physiognomy and strong jaw.

3. Now the drawing begins to turn into a caricature. Notice the introduction of a grin, although he wasn't doing this in the initial drawing. His broad, up-turning grin, intense stare, large bony forehead, nose, cheekbones and jaw are the characteristics the artist has stressed.

EXPERIMENTING

Ultimately, all superfluous lines may be deleted. You can do this more effectively if you know your subject well. You need knowledge to be able to build into your caricature the appropriate attitudes, movements, and favorite expressions in order to inject a bit of humor as well as get across a likeness with a minimum of detail.

See how far you can take the exaggeration before the subject becomes unrecognizable.

Try to capture the obvious features first, and then the general effect of the head or face.

Don't try caricaturing your friends, unless they agree first.

If you can't get the subject you want to pose for you, try to obtain good photographs of them. These won't provide quite as good reference, but as long as you draw on your knowledge of the person as well, they should be adequate.

Identifying features
1. *Round head*
2. *Fat chin*
3. *Thin mouth*
4. *Heavy, anxious eyebrows*
5. *Little eyes with bags*
6. *Swollen or broken nose*
7. *Wrinkles and stubbly chin*

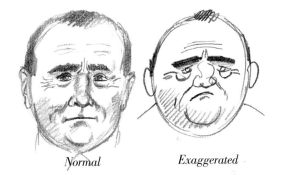

Normal   *Exaggerated*

Identifying features
1. *Round-ended, turned-up nose*
2. *Bright eye*
3. *Thick eyebrows*
4. *Big hair on top*
5. *Chin*
6. *Sly grin*

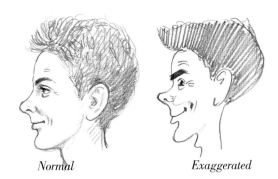

Normal   *Exaggerated*

LESSONS

LESSON 1: STILL LIFE PLANNING YOUR PICTURE

HELPFUL HINT

Make the first two sketches the same size as your finished painting. Ideally the finished sketch should also be the same size, but if it is going to be a larger painting then the finished sketch can be 9" x 12" or 12" x 18".

It is always more enjoyable to paint inspirational subjects and this is often reflected in the quality of the work. Always choose subjects that you feel moved or inspired by. Never just paint a subject for the sake of it. Once you have chosen a subject, a little thought and planning goes a long way in helping ensure that you finish with a successful painting. Sketching plays a very important part in the picture planning stage.

Step 1: Set up a simple still life subject on a table. This example uses a mixing bowl, two eggs, a wooden spoon, a jug and a bag of flour. Step 1 illustrates how to rough out the correct positions of the items in the still life in your sketch.

Step 2: Observe the objects and add more detail to give them a more definite form.

Step3: In the third, far more completed sketch, the direction and strength of the light was chosen, the light, medium and dark tones added, and the darkest features shadows filled in. These three quick sketches will help you get to know the subject and to identify and resolve any problem areas. These preliminary sketches can act as the basis for a painting.

LESSON 2: MONOCHROME WITH PEN AND INK

HELPFUL HINT

Stand your bottle of ink in a clean plastic container. This way, if you happen to catch it with your pen or tip it over, the spills will be contained and easily cleaned.

This demonstration helps you to better understand tone and the role it plays in sketching and painting. When you have tried the demonstration, look for subjects in color and try sketching them using this monochrome technique. The demonstration of the duck in the diagram is an excellent way of recognizing and understanding the value of monochrome studies. Make a tone strip like this one by mixing small amounts of India ink with water on your pallet, adding more water to create the lighter tones and less for the darker tones.

Step 1: Draw the outline of the duck using a 2B pencil.

Step 2: Brush the lightest tone on the duck as shown. Leave white paper for highlights, and let it dry. Apply your medium tone as shown and let dry.

Step 3: Apply your darkest tone last as shown and let dry. To finish, overdraw your pencil lines with pen and ink as shown on the back of this card.

TONAL TEST STRIP

67

LESSON 3: PECKING CHICKENS

HELPFUL HINT

Break your charcoal stick to form a sharp edge when you want to make thin lines for sketching.

Chickens are comical creatures, with their jerky strutting and pecking. See if you can capture their movement in your drawing.

Step 1: Using charcoal, sketch the main shapes with loose, lively marks.

Step 2: To make the feathers in the tails look bold, use large sweeping strokes with the side of your charcoal. Leave the areas where the light plays on the feathers clear. Also darken areas around the heads and faces. Use your finger to blend in areas and make the bodies look round.

Step 3: Build up more detail on body feathers and around the heads and faces. Make bodies and claws stand out by blending shadows under and around them. Sketch in grain and ground details. Use larger marks in the foreground and smaller ones in the background to give a feeling of depth and space.

Step 4: Finish off details around the heads, especially on the combs, beaks and eyes. If you can, sketch animals from life —then you will really capture their spirit.

LESSON 4: SKATEBOARDER

TRY THIS

Practice drawing lines of different weights. When you draw the first lines, keep them light and soft to make them easier to erase. When you get to the final stages, you can increase the pressure on your pencil to make your lines heavier and more definite.

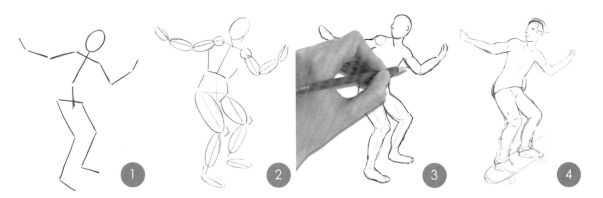

Figure drawing is a lot easier than you think if you start by getting the pose right and fill in the details later.

Step 1: Start with a simple 'stick figure' to get the position of arms and legs correct. The head is an egg shape.

Step 2: Build up the figure using simple shapes. Draw sausages for the arms, legs, hands and feet. Use lines for the torso and hips, and circles for the shoulders. Try to get a feel for body angles and where the weight falls.

Step 3: Join the outlines of the shapes to form a more recognizable figure. You can erase the earlier lines now, or leave them until later.

Step 4: Now sketch in the board and the clothing. The fabric will form folds where the body bends – at the waist and knees, for example. Look at yourself in the mirror to see how your own clothes fall.

Step 5: Erase your guide lines and go over the lines you want to keep. At this stage, you can build up the facial features and other details such as shoes. You can use a few pastels to color in your drawing. Do it quickly and freely, and keep the shading lines sketchy.

LESSON 5: BABY HARE

HELPFUL HINT

A small pad of sandpaper is great for sharpening the charcoal sticks. Use the sandpaper to sharpen the tip of the charcoal to a fine point.

Make light strokes with the sharp edge of your charcoal stick to draw this delicate little hare.

Step 1: Lightly sketch the basic shape: and oval head, banana-shaped ears, and round body. Make a rounded eye, a V-shaped nose, and a gentle curve for the mouth.

Step 2: Start making marks that show the texture of the fur. Build up lines that follow the curves of the hare's body.

Step 3: Continue making light feathered strokes in the direction of the fur, over the head, ears, and body. Add dark to the eye, leaving a white speck for light.

Step 4: Make more fur strokes — cluster some together and follow the body shape.

Step 5: Add dark areas to the inner ear, and between the feet to show the hare's form and bring it to life. Continue with double strokes for the grass, letting them taper off. See how the grass size shows that it is a baby animal. Put whiskers in with a fast flick, not heavy pressure. If the eye does not look bright enough, add a little white pastel.

LESSON 6:
HEAD OF A BOY

TRY THIS

Over your paper, scrape a brown pastel with an old blunt knife or a paper clip. Be careful not to breathe in any of the dust. With paper towel, smear the dust to make a brown color all over. It will be more interesting if the color is not even, so you could add more colors if you wish.

Practice drawing people with this simple sketch.

Step 1: Make an interesting background with brown pastel on white paper.

Step 2: With charcoal outline the simple head and shoulder shapes. Show, with a light mark, the position of the eyes, nose, and mouth. Look at the proportion of the head.

Step 3: Draw features more definitely. Notice that the eyes are not drawn in full, with a line all around them. Only the top lid is shown.

Step 4: Show shadow shapes in the eyes, under the nose, and under the top and bottom lips. Also put in shadows under the chin and the arms. Make strokes for the hair, but don't make them too heavy. Try to get as good a likeness as you can.

Step 5: Look at where the light falls on the face, hair, and shirt. Make highlight shapes with white pastel in strong marks. To finish, give more shape to the nostrils and detail to the eye. Make fine lines for hair and final touches to the T-shirt to mark the collar and sleeves.